D0875965

ALEXANDER HAMILTON

AND

AARON BURR

Joined by Fate:
INTERTWINED BIOGRAPHIES

ALEXANDER
HAMILTON
AND
AARON
BURR

RICHARD WORTH

Enslow Publishing
101 W. 23rd Street
Suite 240
New York, NY 10011
USA

enslow.com

Published in 2019 by Enslow Publishing, LLC.
101 W. 23rd Street, Suite 240, New York, NY 10011

Library of Congress Cataloging-in-Publication Data

Names: Worth, Richard, author.
Title: Alexander Hamilton and Aaron Burr / Richard Worth.
Description: New York : Enslow, 2019. | Series: Joined by fate:
Intertwined biographies | Includes bibliographical references and index.
| Audience: Grades 7 to 12.
Identifiers: LCCN 2017054762| ISBN 9780766098121 (library bound) |
    ISBN 9780766098138 (pbk.)
Subjects: LCSH: Burr-Hamilton Duel, Weehawken, N.J., 1804. | Hamilton, Alexander,
    1757–1804. | Burr, Aaron, 1756–1836. | Statesmen—United States—Biography.
    | Vice-Presidents—United States—Biography. | United States—Politics and
    government—1783–1809. | United States—Politics and government—1775–1783.
Classification: LCC E302.6.H2 W86 2018 | DDC 973.4/60922—dc23
LC record available at https://lccn.loc.gov/2017054762

Printed in the United States of America

To Our Readers: We have done our best to make sure all website addresses in this book
were active and appropriate when we went to press. However, the author and the publisher
have no control over and assume no liability for the material available on those websites or
on any websites they may link to. Any comments or suggestions can be sent by e-mail to
customerservice@enslow.com.

CONTENTS

INTRODUCTION

During the 1700s and 1800s, dueling was one of the ways that gentlemen settled serious disagreements. These "gentlemen" belonged to the upper classes in the United States—large landowners, wealthy merchants, and politicians. For them, honor was among their most cherished possessions. If they believed another gentleman had insulted their honor, they might challenge him to a duel.

The custom of dueling originated in Europe. Between 1760 and 1820, approximately 172 duels were fought in Great Britain, and about 70 of them ended in death. Some of the men who participated in duels included William Pitt, a British prime minister, and Edmund Burke, a British political leader.[1]

In the United States, dueling grew in popularity at about the time of the American Revolution and continued to be practiced for another century. It especially gained a following in the South among wealthy landowners. But why did men agree to participate in duels, even though the contests sometimes ended in death? As Alexander Hamilton, America's most famous duelist, explained, "The ability to be in future useful in those crises [in] public affairs which seem likely to happen…imposed on me (as I thought) a peculiar necessity not to decline the call."[2]

These affairs of honor, as they were called, followed certain rules described in codes of honor. Publications such as *The Dueling Handbook* outlined the rules quite carefully. If one man challenged another to a duel for insulting his honor, his opponent could not turn down the challenge—at least not with his honor intact. Still, a man did not have to agree to take part in a duel right away.

Often, the initial steps involved in prepping for a duel took several weeks, even months, before the duel occurred. For example, one politician might accuse another of theft and falsehoods. The first step might be a demand from the accused asking for an apology. The accuser might then write a response, and from there, the men might exchange several more letters. If they still could not resolve their conflict, then the two men might proceed to a duel. Generally each duelist brought an assistant, known as a second, to the match. Seconds were usually close friends of the duelists. They found places to hold the matches and observed the contests to make sure they followed code.

Before the eighteenth century, men often dueled with swords. But by the 1700s, dueling pistols had replaced swords as preferred weapons, and gentlemen typically owned sets of such pistols. This ensured that each duelist had the same weapon.

When the matches began, both duelists were expected to stand a certain distance from each other. Then, when an observer, or second, gave the signal, duelists could fire their weapons. Usually, neither man suffered fatal wounds—if they were hit at all. But the duel between US Founding Father Alexander Hamilton and politician Aaron Burr was no ordinary contest. Hamilton died during the bout, and Burr lost his honor.

What led the two men to have this deadly encounter? Their life stories shed some light.

DUEL TO THE DEATH

The morning of July 11, 1804, a small boat pushed off from a dock on Manhattan Island in New York and began to cross the Hudson River. It headed for a popular dueling ground called the Heights of Weehawken in New Jersey, about 20 feet (6 meters) above the river. Both New York and New Jersey had outlawed dueling, but New Jersey officials did not strictly enforce the laws.

An Illegal Face-off

The boat carried Aaron Burr, who served as vice president for President Thomas Jefferson. Burr's second, or assistant, William P. Van Ness, accompanied him along with another friend, Matthew L. Davis. After arriving at Weehawken, Van Ness began clearing an area of brush to create the dueling ground.

At about the same time, another boat also headed across the Hudson River from a separate dock in Manhattan. This boat transported Alexander Hamilton, a principal founder of America's government and secretary of the treasury under President George Washington. Hamilton's second, Judge Nathaniel Pendleton, accompanied him along with David Hosack, a Columbia College professor of medicine.

Aaron Burr belonged to one of America's most prominent families. He became a hero of the American Revolution, a famous lawyer in New York, and the third vice president of the United States.

Hamilton arrived shortly after Burr. At about 7 a.m., the two men drew lots, and Hamilton selected the side where he would stand and fire. Each man used a Wogdon dueling pistol from a set owned by Hamilton's brother-in-law. Hamilton's son, Philip, had used these same pistols in a duel fought near Jersey City in 1801. Philip Hamilton defended his father's honor after another man criticized him. Unfortunately, the duel cost Philip Hamilton his life.

Duels were not uncommon in the early American republic. If a man felt that he had been insulted by another, he could demand a duel—an "affair of honor"—to show that he was willing to die to preserve his reputation. But most affairs never reached the actual dueling stage. Instead, the two men would

Dueling with Pistols

Dueling with guns was only made possible because of the development of gunpowder and the use of firearms. Rifles were first used in Europe in the fourteenth century when firearms appeared at the Battle of Crecy in France. Over the next three centuries, rifles became more sophisticated. Flintlock rifles were widely used during wars in Europe in the seventeenth and eighteenth centuries. American settlers and soldiers who fought in the French and Indian War used these same weapons.

By 1750, dueling pistols had replaced swords in Europe and the Americas as the most widely used weapons in the bouts. In 1777, the standard dueling pistol had a 9- or 10-inch (22- or 25-cm) barrel, with a 1-inch (2.54-cm) bore (circumference of the inside of the barrel) and a ball about a quarter of an ounce (7 grams). Some of these pistols had elaborate decorations and ivory handles.

Born in the Caribbean, Alexander Hamilton later immigrated to America, where he became the close friend of George Washington, a hero of the Battle of Yorktown.

negotiate through their seconds by an exchange of letters. There would be a demand for an explanation of the "insult" followed by further negotiations leading to a written apology. And the men would avoid a duel.

Why Hamilton and Burr Clashed

With Hamilton and Burr, negotiations led nowhere. The men shared a long history that led to mutual hatred. When Burr ran for president in the election of 1800, Hamilton led the powerful Federalist Party in opposition to Burr, leading to the election of Thomas Jefferson.

After that, Hamilton helped stop Burr's effort to become New York's governor. He wrote letters that were published in the newspapers attacking Burr's reputation. In retaliation, Burr challenged Hamilton to a duel and demanded an apology. When Hamilton refused to apologize for what he had written, both men arranged to meet at Weehawken.

Still, a match to the death might have been avoided. In many duels, both men simply fired toward the ground. In this way, they had demonstrated their courage but avoided bloodshed. Sadly, this did not occur during the duel between Hamilton and Burr. Hamilton probably fired first, sending his bullet high over Burr's head. Hamilton had decided on this course of action because he did not want to take another man's life in a duel. Burr

Normally duelists fired their guns into the ground to avoid killing their opponent, but Aaron Burr defied this custom, taking Alexander Hamilton's life.

In 1804, Hamilton and Burr met in New Jersey for the most famous duel fought in the United States; Hamilton lost his life, and Burr lost his political reputation and was later tried for treason.

retaliated, taking careful aim and firing a shot that hit Hamilton in the hip, fracturing a rib and entering Hamilton's liver.

"I am a dead man. This is a mortal wound," Hamilton whispered to Hosack.[1] Hosack and Pendleton carried Hamilton to the boat and hoped to bring him back to New York. For a while, Hamilton's pulse could not be detected, according to Hosack, but the doctor eventually revived him. Despite the physician's efforts, Hamilton died from the wound the next day, and Burr fled into hiding.

Hamilton's Funeral

Alexander Hamilton's funeral took place on July 14, 1804, in New York. A group of soldiers accompanied Hamilton's coffin to the cemetery as a band played a funeral march. Gouverneur Morris, a close friend of Hamilton's, a political leader in the new republic, and signer of the Declaration of Independence, gave the funeral oration.

Morris recalled Hamilton's career as a student, his service in the American Revolution, and his work as secretary of the treasury. He said, "At the time when our government was organized, we were without funds, though not without resources. To call them into action, and establish order in the finances, [President] Washington sought for splendid talents, for extensive information, and, above all, he sought for...incorruptible integrity—All these he found in Hamilton."[2]

The duel between Hamilton and Burr brought to a tragic end a bitter rivalry between two men considered leaders of their country. Each had fought valiantly in the American Revolution. Both had devoted themselves to politics, rising to positions of leadership; and each lost everything as a result of a duel. Through their lives weaves the story of the early American republic.

GROWING UP IN THE COLONIES

An island in the Caribbean Sea, Nevis is only about 36 square miles (93 square kilometers). During the 1700s, it became a center of the sugar trade. Enslaved blacks, taken from Africa, grew and harvested sugar cane. Then, they took it to nearby mills where the sugar was squeezed from the cane and formed into large cubes. This made it easier to transport. From there, British sailing ships took the sugar to North America and Europe. Families and tavern owners used sugar to sweeten coffee and tea. Bakeries relied on sugar as a primary ingredient in sweets and pastries. And sugar became a key ingredient in the production of rum.

Alexander Hamilton's Origins

The people living on the island of Nevis included an attractive red-haired woman named Rachel Faucette. She had grown up on a small plantation on the Caribbean island of Saint Croix. Her brother-in-law James Lytton owned the plantation, known as the Grange.

In 1745, while still in her teens, Rachel married a Danish settler named Johan Michael Lavien, who was already thirty. During the five years they were married, Lavien abused his

16

wife until she left him. But he would not give her a divorce and accused Rachel of being unfaithful. The authorities in Saint Croix believed Lavien, and they sent Rachel to prison in Christiansted, the principal settlement on the island.

When Rachel was finally released, she left for nearby St. Kitts, another sugar-rich island. There, she met James Hamilton, the son of a Scots nobleman, and the couple moved to Nevis. They had two children—James and Alexander, who was born in 1755.

About a thousand Europeans lived on the island of Nevis, but the ten thousand enslaved Africans who worked on the plantations vastly outnumbered them. As Alexander grew up, he witnessed how cruelly white slaveholders treated the blacks working their land. Vicious beatings weren't uncommon. One planter, Edward Huggins, whipped a male slave 365 times and a female slave 292 times. Those who survived such lashings often died because of the backbreaking work in the sugar cane fields. In fact, 40 percent of the slaves died within five years.

Alexander faced a number of challenges as a young boy. When he was just seven, his father abandoned the family. Soon afterward, Rachel moved her two sons back to Saint Croix. Although the island boasted an ample amount of sugar cane, it produced little else the people who lived there needed. In 1765, Rachel moved into a house at 34 Company Street, in Christiansted, the capital of St. Croix, where she ran a small store.

As a single mother, Rachel had to earn money for her family. From the merchant ships that came into Christiansted harbor, Rachel bought fish, flour, fruit, and other products she sold to the townspeople. From his mother, Alexander probably learned the basic elements of trade and how to make a profit at selling goods. But the apprenticeship lasted only a short time. Early in 1768, Rachel developed a raging fever and died on February 19.

Hamilton grew up on the tiny Caribbean island of Nevis, known for its large sugar cane plantations worked by thousands of enslaved Africans who made the European settlers rich.

Alexander and his brother were now on their own. They had to fend for themselves as the illegitimate sons of a single mother. Most people in Christiansted looked down on the two young Hamiltons. But the clerks in the local branch of the New York trading firm Beekman and Cruger proved to be the exception. The firm had supplied some of the trade goods to Rachel's store and had observed Alexander's skills as a businessman.

After his mother's death, the firm offered Alexander a job. At age twelve, Alexander found himself in charge of Beekman

and Cruger's St. Croix office. According to historian John Sedgwick, Hamilton "didn't just keep track of paperwork, but handled the negotiations, assigned the cargo, and examined the goods themselves, coming and going, to make sure they were up to standard...All the records had to be set down in faultless penmanship in the leger book... 'Believe me, sir, I dun as hard as is proper,' [Hamilton] assured Cruger."

Alexander worked long hours, almost exhausting himself as a young supervisor. Yet he found time to write about a severe hurricane that hit the island for St. Croix's local newspaper. The article caught the eye of a young clergyman from New York City. Hugh Knox had been sent to the Caribbean, where he spent seventeen years helping his parishioners on the islands.

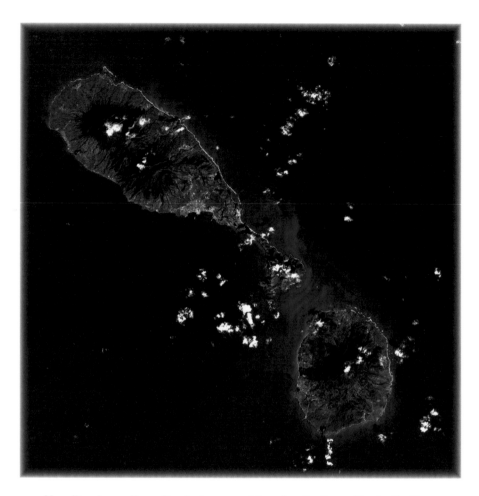

Hamilton's mother, Rachel, moved her family from Nevis (*bottom right*) to nearby St. Kitts (*left*). There, she ran a general store near the harbor of Christiansted, and Alexander learned about business.

After reading Alexander's letter and recognizing the boy's skills, Knox helped gather a small amount of money from his well-to-do friends on the islands. With this money, he offered Alexander a scholarship to Princeton College in New Jersey. It would change his life.

The Early Life of Aaron Burr

By chance, Hugh Knox was also a close friend of Aaron Burr's father, the Rev. Aaron Burr Sr. The elder Burr was a well-known Presbyterian minister in Newark, New Jersey. During the 1730s, after graduating from Yale College in New Haven, Connecticut, Burr got involved in a religious revival called the Great Awakening. A New England minister named Jonathan Edwards spearheaded the movement, which spread across the American colonies.

Edwards was a fiery preacher who held large outdoor revival meetings, attracting hundreds of people. During his sermons, Edwards threatened his followers with eternal hell if they didn't reform their ways. Edwards's sermons not only influenced Burr Sr., but he also became strongly attracted to the preacher's daughter. Esther Edwards was sixteen years younger than Burr. Nevertheless, they eventually married in 1752, when Burr was thirty-six and his wife twenty. Soon afterward, Esther gave birth to a daughter, Sarah. In 1755, the couple welcomed a son, Aaron Burr Jr. By this time, Burr Sr. had not only become a well-known preacher in New Jersey but also president of Princeton College

During the 1750s, the American colonies were in the grip of a bloody war with the French, who controlled Canada. The French and Indian War led to battles in the American wilderness and killings of English settlers on the frontier. The French sent their Native American allies to war with the settlers in hopes of destroying them or forcing them back to the East Coast. In 1757, Aaron Burr Sr. brought young Aaron to Stockbridge, Massachusetts, so the boy could meet his grandfather Jonathan Edwards. Nearby, the French armies besieged Fort William Henry on Lake George.

By the time he returned to Newark, Aaron Burr Sr. developed a high fever and died soon afterward. Esther

The French and Indian War

The French and Indian War (1754–1763) was the final struggle between Great Britain and the French in Canada for control of North America. The war began with a skirmish in the Ohio River Valley between American

colonists, led by Colonel George Washington, and a French expedition. Washington was eventually driven from the battlefield, but a year later the British launched a major invasion of the Ohio Valley aimed at French Fort Duquesne, now Pittsburgh.

Washington led the British retreat from the battlefield after the man he accompanied, General Edward Braddock, was killed. The war then shifted north, with the French winning a series of victories in 1756 and 1757. The French won one victory at Fort William Henry by the base of Lake George in New York.

The Burrs were visiting nearby, a dangerous move since the Native American allies of the French began killing the fort's inhabitants and threatening Massachusetts. Finally, the British navy cut off supplies to the French in Canada. In 1759, the British captured New France's capital, Québec, and took control of Canada.

During the 1750s, the bloody French and Indian War took place in North America. It pitted French Canadians and their Native American allies against the English in a fight for the continent.

The Rev. Aaron Burr Sr. was a well-known preacher. The son-in-law of Jonathan Edwards, Burr served as president of the College of New Jersey, now Princeton.

Burr now found herself alone with two small children. Soon afterward, her father offered to travel to New Jersey and support his daughter and two grandchildren. The illustrious Edwards also took over as Princeton College's president. However, he died after contracting smallpox—a serious disease that took the lives of many people in the 1700s. A short time later, Esther Burr contracted smallpox, dying in April 1758.

Aaron Burr Jr. and his sister, Sarah, called "Sally," suddenly become orphans—much like Alexander Hamilton and his brother had. They went to live with Dr. William Shippen, the physician who had cared for their grandfather, Jonathan Edwards, in Philadelphia. The city wasn't very far from Princeton. Two years later, Shippen handed both Burr children over to their uncle, Timothy Edwards, a merchant in Elizabethtown, New Jersey.

Aaron did not like his uncle Timothy and at four years old decided to run away from home and find a job as a cabin boy on a merchant ship in New York. When his uncle came after him, Aaron climbed up one of the ship's masts but later agreed to come down—probably after Timothy agreed not to punish him for his bad behavior.

Aaron later entered Elizabethtown Academy for boys in New Jersey, where he decided at age eleven that he had learned all the school could teach him. Aaron

> *"The roaring of the sea and wind—fiery meteors flying about in the air—the glare of almost perpetual lightning— the crash of the falling houses—and the ear-piercing shrieks of the distressed, were sufficient to strike astonishment into Angels."*
> **— Alexander Hamilton**

Smallpox

Smallpox is a contagious disease caused by two viruses. People who have it develop a rash characterized by blisters filled with fluid. Up to one-third of the people who caught the disease in colonial America died. In particular, scores of Native Americans died after coming into contact with infected European settlers.

The illness probably arose several thousand years ago. By the 1700s, it killed approximately four hundred thousand people each year. Eventually, researchers developed a vaccine to prevent people from getting the disease. The vaccine became so successful that in the late twentieth century the World Health Organization declared that smallpox had been eliminated.

decided to enter Princeton long before he was old enough to be accepted or had passed the courses necessary to become a freshman. After testing him, the Princeton faculty decided that he was not ready to become a college student.

Aaron vowed to come back and try again. After studying eighteen hours a day to learn all he could in Latin, the Bible, rhetoric, and logic, he passed the Princeton College entrance exams a year later and became a student. Princeton became an institution where many well-to-do families sent their sons to be educated. It was one of the best-known colleges in the colonies. There, Burr's friends included James Madison, who later became the fourth US president.

Burr graduated from Princeton in 1770 at age fifteen. Three years later, Alexander Hamilton would sail into New York and begin his career at the same college.

THE CAULDRON OF THE REVOLUTION

England's victory in the French and Indian War changed the entire political situation in North America. Not only had the British taken control of Canada, they had eliminated the French threat in the Ohio River Valley. This meant that American colonists could move farther west, searching for fertile new lands along the Ohio.

Divisions Between the Colonies and England

But what the British gave with one hand, they took away with the other. In 1763, the English government passed a new law preventing the colonists from moving very far west. Quite simply, England did not want to move troops into the area to defend it. The cost was far too high, and the government in London reasoned that it had already spent enough money to win the war.

In fact, London had already decided to impose new taxes on the colonists to help pay for the cost of winning such a great victory. The colonists, however, saw things quite differently. They had fought alongside the British to win the victory over the French. Many colonists reasoned that since they had no representation in the British Parliament, the government had

no right to impose taxes on them. Throughout the 1760s, as Great Britain tried to introduce one kind of tax after another, the colonists resisted and the British backed down. Parliament removed the taxes but made it clear it could pass a new tax in the future.

Finally, Parliament imposed a tax on imported tea in the early 1770s. In Boston, a group of colonials, calling themselves the Sons of Liberty and dressed as Native Americans, dumped the tea into Boston Harbor. The British government immediately retaliated by closing the port of Boston, which would have destroyed the livelihood of many Massachusetts merchants, sailors, and tradespeople.

In response, Massachusetts informed the colonials who'd agreed to send representatives to the First Continental Congress in Philadelphia in 1774.

Tensions were building in the British colonies when the ship carrying Alexander Hamilton from St. Croix arrived in New

When Hamilton arrived in New York in 1773, relations between Britain and its American colonies had worsened and would soon reach the breaking point that led to revolution two years later.

York Harbor a year earlier. When he disembarked, Hamilton saw one of the largest and busiest cities in America. Pedestrians and horse-drawn carriages crowded the streets of lower Manhattan. Sailing ships in the harbor unloaded huge quantities of imported goods, and crates journeyed from the piers to the shops lining city streets. Hamilton had never seen a city bustling with so much activity, certainly not in tiny Nevis or St. Croix.

After arriving in New York, Hamilton hoped to journey to Princeton to begin his higher education. But he soon realized, like Aaron Burr, that he needed more training to pass the courses offered during his freshman year. So, just as Burr did, Hamilton headed south to Elizabethtown Academy. Fortunately, through Knox, he connected with some important people in New York,

Hamilton received a scholarship to Princeton, where Burr had been a student several years earlier. Ultimately, Hamilton decided to attend King's College, which later became Columbia University.

Hamilton's Poem

Alexander Hamilton wrote a poem to commemorate the death of Elias Boudinot's young daughter, Anna Maria.

> For the sweet babe, my doting heart
> Did all a mother's fondness feel;
> Careful to act each tender part
> And guard from every threatening ill
> But what, alas, availed my care:
> The unrelenting hand of death,
> Regardless of a parent's prayer
> Has stopped my lovely infant's breath.[1]

including William Livingston. Livingston belonged to one of the nation's wealthiest families and invited Hamilton to live at his spacious home, Liberty Hall, in New Jersey.

There, Hamilton mingled with other elite families and even struck up a relationship with two of Livingston's sisters: Catherine and Sarah. He also met Elias Boudinot, leader of the American Bible Society. Hamilton grew so close to the family that when Boudinot's young daughter died, Hamilton wrote a poem about her death. While infant mortality was quite common during this time, it didn't make a parent's loss any easier.

When Hamilton grew strong enough academically to enter Princeton, something unforeseen occurred. He found that the political situation in the American colonies affected colleges as much as other parts of society. Princeton was a hotbed of opposition to English rule. But Hamilton, who had lived his entire life in British colonies, fiercely supported the English Crown. As a result of his loyalty to Great Britain, he decided to continue his education elsewhere. One of his contacts in New Jersey helped Hamilton find a place at King's College in lower Manhattan—a place where he found many other students loyal to England.

The Coming Revolution

As Hamilton pursued higher education at King's College, Aaron Burr set out to find a satisfying career. At first, Burr thought he might be suited to life as a clergyman, like his illustrious father and grandfather, so he attended a seminary for training.

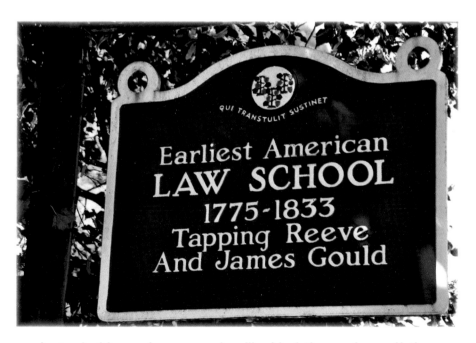

Instead of becoming a preacher like his father and grandfather, Aaron Burr decided to become a lawyer and attend classes at Litchfield Law School, the first law school in the United States.

But the education bored him, and Burr decided to try law instead. In 1774, he attended the first law school established in the American colonies. An old friend of Burr, Tapping Reeve, opened the school in Litchfield, Connecticut. Reeve was also married to Aaron's sister, Sally.

While Burr attended law school, Hamilton adjusted to American life, and his opinions about American defiance of the British Parliament began to change. As he listened to debates in New York about the closing of Boston port and other colonial grievances, Hamilton eventually found himself speaking out in favor of the settlers. He even began writing pamphlets expressing his opinions.

For Burr and Hamilton, respectively, legal training and a college degree from King's College seemed far less important than the startling news coming out of Massachusetts. In April 1775, at Lexington and Concord, British regulars had clashed with a group of colonial volunteers, called Minutemen. These Minutemen had chased the soldiers of the world's greatest army back into Boston. Then, the Minutemen began to lay siege to the British forces inside the city.

When Burr heard the news, he immediately headed for Boston to join the Continental army gathered there. General George Washington, appointed by the Continental Congress, commanded the army. Burr yearned to participate in a battle but saw no action because he fell ill soon after his arrival. His sickness led him to miss out on the Battle of Bunker Hill, fought in June 1775.

Burr, though, recovered in time to volunteer for another expedition. This one was heading toward Canada to conquer Montréal and Québec, then under Great Britain's control. Two small, separate American armies had been assigned to march toward Canada, which America's leaders believed would be a natural fit for an independent North American nation.

When the revolution broke out, Burr left law school and joined General Richard Montgomery's expedition to capture Québec and Montréal in Canada. But they failed, and Montgomery was killed.

One army, commanded by General Richard Montgomery, headed for Montréal. The other, commanded by Colonel Benedict Arnold, sailed from Newburyport, Massachusetts, north of Boston, to southern Maine. Then the troops headed inland on large rafts, along the Kennebec River, across the Dead River, and finally to the banks of the St. Lawrence River, just across from Québec. Burr traveled with this small army.

The expedition began easily enough as the soldiers floated down the Kennebec, traveling through a multicolored forest during a beautiful September. But eventually the men reached the Great Carrying Place, where they had to carry their barges. They experienced heavy rains, swampy trails, and eventually much colder weather. Although the men fished for trout that sustained them, the army ran out of bread. The rains grew worse, and a giant storm sent trees falling to the ground as the rivers flooded everything along the way.

The teaming rivers destroyed many of the barges, called bateaux, and barrels of food washed away. Burr and his fellow soldiers had never anticipated that war would be so brutal. According to historian Christopher Ward, the soldiers "boiled and roasted moccasins, shot pouches and old leather breeches, and chewed on them. They killed the captain's Newfoundland dog and ate all but the bones, which they kept for soup."[2]

Ward added that on November 9, 1775, the people living on "the bank of the St. Lawrence saw, emerging from the woods, a band of scarecrows, their clothing 'torn in pieces.'" Only six hundred of the eleven hundred men who had started the journey arrived in Canada, a trip that had taken forty-five days and covered 350 miles (563 km). As Ward wrote, "Arnold's journey to Québec is one of the most famous military marches recorded in history...For sustained courage, undaunted resolution, and uncomplaining endurance of almost incredible hardships, those

After a long march north, American troops attacked Québec during a huge blizzard. Burr endured great hardships during the march, and the weather conditions forced the soldiers to retreat.

> *"For sustained courage, undaunted resolution, and uncomplaining endurance of almost incredible hardships, those men who grimly persisted to the end [in the march to Quebec] deserved high honor and unstinted praise."*

men who grimly persisted to the end deserved high honor and unstinted praise."[3]

One of those men was young Aaron Burr. He had bravely lived through the hardships of an incredible expedition. But now the men had to capture the heavily defended fortress of Québec. Meanwhile, General Montgomery had taken control of Montréal and now headed south with most of his men to reinforce Colonel Arnold.

When Montgomery arrived, he brought another three hundred soldiers. He also brought artillery to bombard the walls of Québec and heavy clothing for Montgomery's soldiers. It was now December, the snows in Canada were very heavy, and the temperature was frigidly cold. Finally, at the end of December, in the face of a blinding blizzard, the troops attacked. But the weather and the British defenses were too much for them. As Montgomery raised his sword and led a charge against defenders, artillery fire from inside Québec killed him. And hundreds of others were killed, wounded, or captured.

Burr was right next to Montgomery as he was shot, and he carried the general's body back to the American camp. The assault on Québec had ended in failure. While Burr was proud of the way he had performed during the campaign, it did nothing to change the outcome.

The Death of Montgomery

With his death, Richard Montgomery became one of the first American heroes of the Revolution. In 1777, a schoolteacher at Maryland's Somerset Academy named Hugh Henry Breckenridge crafted a stage drama of the Québec attack. It became a well-known piece of literature during the American Revolution.

Born in Scotland in 1748, Breckenridge came to Pennsylvania with his family at age five. He attended Princeton, like Burr and Hamilton before him. After studying religion, Breckenridge joined George Washington's army during the Revolution, where he served as chaplain. Later he became a lawyer and moved west to Pittsburgh, becoming founder of the city's first newspaper, the *Pittsburgh Gazette.* Over the next few years, he published sections of a novel called *Modern Chivalry,* which he finished in 1815, a year before his death. Critics considered it the first important novel about the American West.

Hamilton in New York and Pennsylvania

While Burr marched to Canada, Hamilton remained in New York. Without finishing college, he joined the New York regiment of continental soldiers, where he became an artillery officer. Hamilton recruited a group of men that he molded into an artillery regiment. They guarded the tip of Manhattan against a British fleet, expected to appear at almost any moment to attack the city.

Indeed, just as American political leaders were signing the Declaration of Independence in Philadelphia, the powerful British navy sailed into the East River along the shores of

Manhattan. By this time, Hamilton had taken up a position alongside other Continental soldiers in Brooklyn Heights, Long Island, across the water from Manhattan. In July, under the command of General Sir William Howe, thousands of British troops put to shore on eastern Long Island and marched toward the Continental army.

What started as a battle soon became a rout, as Howe led his men around the flank of the American defenders. Many were shot and bayoneted by advancing British troops. Washington's army was lucky to escape back across the East River, through New York and northward. From there, they hastily retreated across the Hudson River, through New Jersey and across the Delaware River into Pennsylvania.

Hamilton and his artillery company retreated with the army. Continental soldiers had enlisted for only a short period of time, and when their enlistments were up at the end of 1776, they intended to go home. The Americans appeared to be no match for the well-trained British soldiers, and there seemed little point in continuing the conflict.

General Washington desperately needed a victory to convince his soldiers to stay with him. And on Christmas Eve 1776, he took the greatest gamble of his military career. With the few thousand troops he had left, Washington crossed the icy waters of the Delaware River, where he surprised a British outpost in Trenton, New Jersey, on Christmas morning. German troops, called Hessians, manned the post, but after a night of Yuletide cheer they were in no condition to fight.

Surprised by the American army, they did not put up much of a battle. Hamilton led his artillery company during the short encounter, firing rounds of shots into the Hessian camp. After the victory at Trenton, Washington further surprised the British high command by marching inland to Princeton. There, a few days later, the Continental army won another victory. This time Hamilton led his artillery company against a detachment of enemy troops holed up inside a building, which led them to surrender.

After the battles, the army traveled 40 miles (64 km) into the hills to spend the winter at an encampment in Morristown, New Jersey. Armies generally stopped fighting during the winter, which was why Washington's march against Trenton and Princeton surprised the British. That winter, General Washington asked Hamilton to join his staff. Although Hamilton was young, Washington recognized that he was a bright and capable soldier. It didn't hurt that he and Hamilton immediately hit it off, developing a friendship that grew over time.

Hamilton soon became Washington's secretary and principal aide—a post he held for almost the entire war.

THE WORLD TURNED UPSIDE DOWN

The year 1777 had a peculiar nickname. People called it the year of the hangman because each "7" looked like a gibbet or scaffold on which the British might hang a rope to execute an American rebel. As his spies watched Lord William Howe in New York, General George Washington tried to figure out where the British might make their next strike. Then, during the late summer, before Washington had fully realized what was happening, Howe left a small force in the city and sailed south with the rest of his army. His target was the American capital, Philadelphia. In European conflicts, once the enemy's capital was captured, the war generally ended. So Howe confidently expected to complete the war with a great victory by the end of the year.

Washington rapidly moved his army south to defend Philadelphia before Howe could reach it. And Hamilton went with him as the general's private secretary and aide. While he yearned for a battlefield command, Hamilton realized that Washington found him far too valuable to transfer him to the field. He needed Hamilton's intelligence and his organizational skills at headquarters.

Meanwhile, Burr had been more fortunate in achieving the battlefield command that he wanted. Earlier in the war, Burr had hoped for the same type of position that Hamilton had achieved—a staff job as an aide to General Washington. But Washington did not like Burr. Instead, Burr had been assigned to the staff of General Israel Putnam and saw action at the Battle of Long Island in 1776. A man who liked action, Burr eventually transferred to a new regiment called the Malcolms.

During this time, the main Continental army had taken up a defensive position along the Brandywine River, near Philadelphia, in September 1777. There, on September 11, Washington's forces awaited the British advance. The soldiers expected the British and their Hessian allies to make a strong frontal attack across several of the fords along the Brandywine.

Once again, General Howe proved to be more than a match for Washington. Leaving the Hessians in front of the river,

The Malcolms

The Malcolms regiment was the brainchild of William Malcolm, a wealthy New York merchant, who paid for the cost of uniforms and other military equipment. But Malcolm knew nothing about commanding men in battle, so he welcomed Burr into his regiment to train the Malcolms and lead them on the battlefield.

Meanwhile, Malcolm was content to return to his business and leave Burr in charge. He succeeded almost right away—training and drilling the Malcolms until they became an effective fighting force. Then, Burr led the regiment in a few skirmishes against the British outposts in New Jersey. He did so well that other men were eager to join the regiment.

General Sir William Howe and his brother Admiral Richard Howe led the British forces in North America during the early years of the war. They won numerous victories.

During the fall of 1781, George Washington led American and French troops in an attack against General Charles Cornwallis's British forces in Yorktown. He forced Cornwallis's surrender.

Howe took the rest of his army in a long flanking movement around the American front lines. Too late, the American high command realized what was happening. As the British troops advanced toward the Continental army, one observer reported seeing General Charles Cornwallis, Howe's second in command, leading the soldiers in their march into battle.

"He was on horseback, appeared tall and sat very erect," the person said. "His rich scarlet clothing loaded with gold lace… occasioned him to make a brilliant and martial appearance." By contrast, General Howe was "a large, portly man, of coarse features. He appeared to have lost his teeth, as his mouth had fallen in."[1] Eventually, the battle began with musket fire and bayonet charges by the British regulars. Outflanked and outnumbered, the Americans gradually retreated and were driven from the battlefield.

General Washington sent Hamilton into Philadelphia to "procure from the inhabitants, contributions of blankets and clothing and materials." But an observer noted that the "sly Tories hid their goods the moment the thing took wind." And Hamilton found few supplies.[2]

The British soon occupied Philadelphia. But Howe was disappointed to discover that the Continental Congress had already fled and had no intention of ending the war and surrendering to Great Britain.

The Winter of Discontent

That winter, the British enjoyed the Christmas holidays in the warm, cozy homes of Philadelphia Tories, residents who supported the British cause. Washington and his troops, on the other hand, spent a cold, miserable winter at Valley Forge. Many of the soldiers had no boots and lacked warm clothing as they shivered in their tents and rundown cabins. Before long, however, they received good news from the north.

After multiple American losses, including the defeat at Brandywine and Germantown, General Washington, Alexander Hamilton, and other US troops spent the winter at Valley Forge, Pennsylvania.

In October, a Continental army commanded by General Horatio Gates and General Benedict Arnold had defeated a large British invading force from Canada. The victory at Saratoga, north of Albany, had electrified Europe, especially the French. The Continentals had proven that they could stand up to the best the British could send against them. And France, which had been secretly supplying the Americans, now declared war on Great Britain, hoping to avenge France's loss in the French and Indian War.

From the American point of view, Prussian military officer Baron Frederick von Steuben's leadership stood out as the only bright spot with regard to Valley Forge. A veteran of many European campaigns, von Steuben drilled the American soldiers day after day, teaching them European tactics and how to face British musket fire and bayonet charges.

That summer at Monmouth Courthouse in New Jersey, the Continentals had the opportunity to put their new training to the test. General Howe had decided to abandon Philadelphia after realizing that its capture had not ended the war. He marched his army north during summer 1778, back to New York. General Washington resolved to catch Howe on the march and defeat his troops in battle.

Washington's advance troops caught the British at Monmouth Courthouse. However, Washington's commander in charge of the advance, General Charles Lee, refused to press the British hard enough. Instead, he retreated from the battle. Washington ran into Lee on the battlefield, and, after finding out what was happening, cursed him "till the leaves shook on the trees," according to one eyewitness. Washington ordered his men forward, with Hamilton by his side, giving out orders. He was "tearing this way and that, urging some troops on, instructing others to pull back, until finally his horse was shot out from under him, and he was pitched forward to the ground...["3]

In 1778, General Cornwallis left Philadelphia to head for New York. Along the way, the British and American armies clashed at the Battle of Monmouth in New Jersey, where Hamilton saw action.

Burr at Monmouth

Aaron Burr also fought at the Battle of Monmouth, leading his Malcolms against the enemy. During the engagement, however, Burr was severely hurt during an artillery bombardment. He later asked Washington if he could "retire from pay and duty" until his recovery. That happened in November 1778.

Burr later returned to active duty, acting as a scout and collecting information about the British activities around New York. About this same time, Burr went back to Elizabethtown where he met Margaret Moncrieff, the daughter of a British officer. At first, Burr found himself strongly attracted to Moncrieff and even invited her to stay at his headquarters. Then, he realized that she might be a spy for the British. So she was placed under house arrest and eventually sent back to her father in New York.[4]

But the battle continued, ending in a draw, and Washington finally let the British leave the battlefield and march north. The Americans had won a morale victory, and Hamilton had seen battlefield action.

Victory at Last

As Burr recovered from his injuries at Monmouth, General Howe led his soldiers back to New York. Thoroughly exhausted from his command in America, Howe had decided to resign and return to England. The new commander in chief was General Henry Clinton, one of Howe's commanders in New York, who decided to open a new campaign in the South.

The southern states—Georgia, as well as North and South Carolina—were the scene of a fierce civil war between loyalists and patriots. Late in 1779, General Clinton sailed south with General Cornwallis and 8,500 men. Their mission was to organize the loyalists and, along with the British troops, take complete control of the South. During the spring of 1780, Clinton laid siege to Charleston, South Carolina. Although strongly defended, the city along the coast fell to the British in May.

From there, British troops struck inland, inflicting a severe defeat on the American forces at Camden, North Carolina, in August. "Never was victory more complete, or defeat more total," said one critic of the battle. General Gates, the victor of Saratoga in 1777, lost almost his entire force of 4,000 men.[5]

To rescue the situation, Washington sent a new general, Nathaniel Greene, to the South. A veteran of the northern campaigns, Greene rebuilt the American army. Then he directed a series of successful campaigns against General Cornwallis that eventually pushed him out of the Carolinas into Virginia in 1781.

Hamilton longed to become involved in the campaign. He'd grown impatient with his desk job on Washington's staff. And in early 1781, Hamilton and Washington had a serious disagreement at Continental army headquarters on the Hudson River. While he had become an essential member of Washington's staff, Hamilton could no longer stand the job. "I hate congress—I hate the army—I hate the world—I hate myself," he wrote.[6]

Hamilton resigned from his position, vowing never to return. He was a man of action, so the inaction

> *"Never was victory more complete or defeat more total."*

of his work had overwhelmed him. Hamilton's personal life may have been another reason for his resignation. Approximately a year earlier, he had met Betsey Schuyler, daughter of General Philip Schuyler. Betsey was beautiful and intelligent, with a very wealthy father. She seemed to combine all the qualities that Hamilton wanted in a wife. On December 14, 1780, they wed, and Hamilton hoped to spend more time with his bride.

But the war continued. Cornwallis retreated to Yorktown, Virginia, along the coast, where the British fleet could protect his army of six thousand men. While the American army had no fleet large enough to challenge the British, their ally, France, did.

In August, Washington received word from French admiral François Joseph Paul de Grasse. His fleet, de Grasse said,

Alexander Hamilton led a brave charge against the British in Yorktown. His efforts led General Cornwallis to surrender and major fighting in North America to come to a close.

was sailing north from the French islands in the Caribbean to Chesapeake Bay, Virginia, outside Yorktown. From his headquarters in New York, Washington decided to head south with his army as quickly as possible to trap Cornwallis.

Hamilton returned to the army and asked General Washington for a field command. Washington, who still liked and respected Hamilton, agreed. Hamilton commanded a brigade of soldiers that marched with the army on their journey south, eventually taking up a position outside Yorktown. Washington's army, which greatly outnumbered the British, began digging trenches and laying siege to Yorktown. On the night of October 14, Hamilton led his brigade in a bayonet charge that overran an important British position, sealing them inside the town.

As Cornwallis wrote to Clinton in New York: "My situation now becomes very critical; we dare not show a gun to their old [artillery] batteries, and I expect that their new ones [from the captured British position] will open tomorrow morning."[7] He feared that the parapets of his defensive position at Yorktown would soon become impossible to defend.

> *"My situation now becomes very critical."*
> — **Charles Cornwallis**

Meanwhile, De Grasse and his men had defeated the British fleet, sealing Yorktown from the Chesapeake Bay. French ships now controlled this escape route for Cornwallis's army. On October 19, 1781, General Cornwallis surrendered. As Hamilton watched from his horse, the British soldiers stacked their weapons on the ground and marched out of Yorktown with their band playing, "The World Turned Upside Down."

THE LAW AND THE CONSTITUTION

While Alexander Hamilton was leading the American charge against the British redoubts in Yorktown, Aaron Burr had already left the army. Burr moved to Albany, New York, to complete his legal education. From Albany, he carried on a long-distance relationship with a New Jersey woman named Theodosia Bartow Prevost.

When the American Revolution broke out in 1775, Bartow Prevost found herself in a very uncomfortable position. She was a patriot, while her husband, Jacques Marcus Prevost, and his friends were members of the British army. This was not unusual in America during the war, when families often split along patriot and loyalist lines. Bartow Prevost lived in a spacious home in New Jersey, called the Hermitage. And, while her husband was away with the army, she hosted patriot leaders such as George Washington.

Washington, along with Aaron Burr, stayed at Bartow Prevost's home after the Battle of Monmouth in 1778. Following the battle, Burr was assigned to accompany Bartow Prevost back to the British stronghold where she could be reunited with her husband. But the British high command had ordered Colonel

Prevost south to join the army in Georgia. Later he left the army in the South and went to the Caribbean, where he served on the British island of Jamaica.

Meanwhile, Bartow Prevost and Burr found themselves developing a close relationship. Their interests were similar, and Burr appreciated her impressive intellect. Their relationship continued when Bartow Prevost returned to her home in New Jersey, and Burr continued to visit her. Earlier, Burr had developed an interest in another English woman, Margaret Moncrieff. But Bartow Prevost was quite different.

Theodosia Bartow

Theodosia Bartow was born in 1746, making her ten years older than Aaron Burr. Her father, Theodosius Bartow, was a successful attorney in New Jersey. And her mother, Ann Sands Stillwell, came from a family who'd lived in America almost since the start of the first colonial settlements. Theodosius died before his daughter was born, leaving his widow to raise her alone. But five years after his death, Ann married Philip de Visme, a captain in the British army.

When Theodosia was seventeen, she also married a British army officer, Lieutenant Colonel Jacques Marcus Prevost. Her two sisters married British officers as well. In colonial America, the wives of British officers often held important positions in society.

Theodosia was unusual for women of her generation, however, and quite different from the rest of her class. Most were content to stay in the background, engaged in needlework, playing a musical instrument, raising children, and hosting parties. But Theodosia was interested in the latest books, the artwork of well-known painters, and colonial politics.

She was older, more mature, and an intellectual. Burr was smitten with her. Late in 1778, he wrote his sister that Bartow Prevost had an "honest and affectionate heart." One of Burr's friends also commented, following his regular visits to the Hermitage, that "she had become the "object of [Burr's] Affections."[1]

The couple was criticized for carrying on an affair, as Bartow was still the wife of a British officer. And some may have even doubted Burr's loyalty to the American cause. Then in 1780, a letter informed Bartow Prevost that Colonel Prevost died of yellow fever in the Caribbean. Two years later, Aaron Burr married Theodosia Bartow Prevost at the Hermitage.

Lawyers in New York City

When he married, Burr was already licensed to practice law in New York. Alexander Hamilton had also decided to leave the army after Yorktown and become a lawyer, completing his education in Albany, as Burr had done. Then in 1783, the United States and Great Britain signed the Treaty of Paris, formally ending the war. The British army left New York City and sailed homeward, taking the loyalists with them.

These loyalists included many lawyers, leaving a demand for new ones in Manhattan. Hamilton and Burr both headed there to set up legal practices in the city. At this time, most residents lived on the tip of Manhattan Island. Hamilton, his wife, Betsey, and their tiny son, Philip, moved into an apartment at 57 Wall Street.

At almost the same time, Burr moved to Manhattan and into a house on Wall Street. Although the Burrs lived just a short distance from the Hamiltons, they did not become friendly. Instead, Burr and Hamilton often found themselves on different sides of the same legal case. With many loyalist lawyers gone, their legal work grew quickly.

Elizabeth Schuyler married Alexander Hamilton during the war. She was the daughter of Philip Schuyler, an American general and political leader.

Since both men were ambitious and eager to make a substantial income, they frequently argued cases against each other and in the same courtroom. One of their colleagues in New York, General Erastus Root, referred to Hamilton and Burr as "the two greatest men in the state, perhaps the nation."[2] While Hamilton stood out for his flowery language in the courtroom, Burr gained a reputation for getting straight to the point. Both men knew how to gather evidence in support of their clients and present it convincingly.

With much of the money he earned, Burr spent lavishly to turn his Manhattan home into one of the most beautiful in the city. As a result, he was often in debt. This forced him to take on as many cases as possible, frequently charging large sums in legal fees. Burr also tried to supplement his income through land speculation—buying pieces of property in hopes of later selling them at huge profits. But that venture never really took off. By the mid-1780s, Burr owed "about $80,000 dollars," according to Hamilton.[3] This was a huge amount of money for that period—equivalent to about eight years of legal earnings.

America at Risk

While Hamilton and Burr were trying to build up their legal practices in New York, the new American nation seemed to be crumbling. During the Revolution, the Continental Congress functioned as the central government, directing the war. But the Congress lacked power and had to beg each of the states for money and soldiers. The individual states retained most of the political control because they feared that any central government might become as powerful as Britain's Parliament.

After the war ended, the weakness of the Continental Congress created serious problems for the new nation. Congress lacked the power to impose taxes to pay for the government or

James Madison was one of America's Founding Fathers, an author of the Federalist Papers that led to the US Constitution, and a Democratic-Republican Party leader. He opposed Hamilton.

sign trade agreements with European nations. Congress could not raise a standing army or protect settlers on the frontier from raids by Native American tribes.

Some of America's leaders, like James Madison of Virginia, recognized the problems with a weak central government. Led by Madison and George Washington, the states sent delegates to a Maryland convention in 1786 to strengthen the central government. Delegates included Alexander Hamilton, who supported changes in the Articles of Confederation to allow Congress to have more influence.

While the convention was meeting, a rebellion broke out in Massachusetts and other states. It was called Shays's Rebellion after leader Daniel Shays. Massachusetts was one of the states proposing to raise taxes to pay for operating the government. Farmers unable to pay the increased taxes faced imprisonment and loss of their farms. When the rebellious farmers tried to capture a military arsenal and seize its weapons, Massachusetts sent out the state militia and squashed the rebellion.

Shays's Rebellion signaled to the delegates in Annapolis, Maryland, that the central government was too weak to handle an uprising that threatened national security. So, they called for another convention to deal with the weaknesses of the Articles of Confederation. The state legislatures selected new delegates to meet in Philadelphia in 1787. Participants included Madison, Hamilton and Washington, chosen by the other delegates to head the convention. During the sweltering heat of summer, the men met and debated the future of the American government. Hamilton favored a strong executive branch, but many delegates opposed this idea and accused him of wanting a king.

Small states and large states also wrangled over the makeup of a federal legislature. States such as Delaware and Connecticut feared that large states, like Pennsylvania or Virginia, might have too much power in the legislature and dictate new laws

In the 1780s, Daniel Shays led Massachusetts farmers to rebel against higher taxes there. The rebellion also revealed the weakness of the American central government.

The Constitutional Convention brought together some of the best minds in America, including Benjamin Franklin, George Washington, James Madison, and Alexander Hamilton.

to the smaller, weaker states. Finally, the delegates worked out a compromise. It included a legislature with two houses—one based on population, favoring the large states, and one with the same number of elected representatives from each state—preserving the power of the smaller states.

When the convention finally adjourned, it had not simply amended the Articles of Confederation. The delegates had created a new constitution to govern America. But for the new document to go into effect, a two-thirds majority of the states had to approve it.

Madison, Hamilton and another New York delegate, John Jay, began writing a series of letters that were published in local newspapers throughout the states. Called the Federalist Papers, they presented strong arguments in favor of adopting the new constitution.

In *Federalist No. 6,* Hamilton wrote to the people of New York: "A man must be far gone…who can seriously doubt that, if [the] States should either be wholly disunited, or only united in partial confederacies, the subdivisions into which they might be thrown would have frequent and violent contests with each other. To presume a want of motives of such contests as an argument against their existence, would be to forget that men are ambitious, vindictive, and rapacious. To look for a continuation of harmony between a number of independent, unconnected sovereignties in the same neighborhood, would be to disregard the uniform course of human events, and to set at defiance the accumulated experience of ages."[4]

Although Hamilton presented eloquent reasons for supporting the new Constitution, many Americans opposed it. They feared a powerful central government that might place heavy taxes on them like England's Parliament had done

How the Delegates Voted on Ratification

Even today, debates continue about how much influence large states and small states should have in this country. After the 2016 presidential election, for example, calls increased for the nation to disband or update the Electoral College. Disagreements also go on about the rights of states versus the rights of the federal government.

How might you have voted on ratifying the Constitution? Here's how the delegates did.

State	For	Against
Delaware	30	0
Pennsylvania	46	23
New Jersey	38	0
Georgia	26	0
Connecticut	128	40
Massachusetts	187	168
Rhode Island	16	48
Maryland	63	11
South Carolina	149	73
New Hampshire	57	47
Virginia	89	79
New York	30	27
North Carolina	79	193

Rhode Island and North Carolina eventually ratified the Constitution after the Bill of Rights was added to the original document.

> *"I shall now proceed to delineate dangers...which will in all probability flow from the dissensions between the States themselves, and from domestic factions and convulsions."*
> —Alexander Hamilton, *Federalist No. 6.*

during the 1770s. The opposition was especially strong in New York, where Governor George Clinton led a powerful group against ratification.

But many states included residents who supported the Constitution. The delegates to state conventions debated and voted on the Constitution from the end of 1787 to mid-1788. And two-thirds of the states voted in favor. America had a new government.

THE INDISPENSABLE MAN

In April 1789, President George Washington crossed the Hudson River on a magnificent barge. He received a thirteen-gun salute when he arrived in New York City, the federal capital. For the new nation, Washington was a hero. He had kept the Continental army together against long odds, finally winning a decisive victory at Yorktown. He had presided over the Constitutional Convention in Philadelphia. And most Americans approved the new Constitution because they believed Washington would be the first president. They then elected him overwhelmingly in 1788, with John Adams as his vice president.

If Washington was indispensable to the new nation, Alexander Hamilton had become indispensable to Washington. He had served as his secretary and aide during the war and led a charge against the British that turned the course of the battle at Yorktown. So, in 1789, President Washington appointed Hamilton to the most important position in his cabinet, secretary of the treasury. Although the new Constitution brought the thirteen states together, the nation would not survive unless the federal government could stabilize America's finances.

Hamilton needed to make sure this happened as quickly as possible. He lacked the training of a longtime banker, like

State conventions approved the new Constitution in part because they were sure George Washington, a man widely admired, would serve as the nation's first president.

Robert Morris who had directed America's finances during the Revolutionary War. But Hamilton had common sense, and his work in trading operations as a young man had taught him important lessons about finance. He was willing to work around the clock to get the job done.

The New Administration

During the Revolutionary War, Congress had issued bonds to pay soldiers and purchase military supplies. American citizens purchased the bonds with the understanding that Congress would pay back the bonds at full value plus interest. But the government was broke after the war ended, so the people who'd bought bonds sold them at less than face value to speculators. These speculators gambled that the bonds might eventually be paid off for what they were worth.

When he became treasury secretary, Hamilton reasoned that the federal government had to fulfill its promise to honor the bonds at full value. Otherwise, the government would lose the public's trust and be unable to borrow money for future projects. This meant that the speculators would now reap the rewards of the bonds, and the original owners—some of them soldiers who had fought in the Revolution—would not receive any financial reward. Hamilton's decision made sense for the future financial credit of the US government, but it faced a backlash from Americans who had already sold off their bonds.

In a second decision, Hamilton decided that the government should also pay off the debts states had accumulated to pay their soldiers during the Revolution. This would benefit northern states, which had run up larger debts to pay for the war because the Revolution began earlier there, resulting in more battles in the region.

Hamilton's decision outraged the South, which had already paid off its debts. Led by Thomas Jefferson and James Madison

Thomas Jefferson became the first secretary of state, but he soon clashed with Alexander Hamilton about the best way to set the nation on firm financial footing.

of Virginia, southern states tried to stop Hamilton from carrying out his plan. While Hamilton insisted that this decision further strengthened the financial credit of the new nation, Madison and Jefferson claimed it was unfair to the South.

Finally, they reached a compromise. Over dinner one evening, the three men came to an agreement. Madison and Jefferson would support Hamilton's program, but in turn, he would persuade his followers in Congress to support a plan to move the federal capital south in the next ten years to Washington, DC.

Hamilton, Burr, and New York Politics

Hamilton was not only secretary of the treasury. He also filled an important role in New York politics. His father-in-law was

The Deal

Although Hamilton agreed to a new location for the nation's capital, he never forgot the opposition of the two Virginians. As he wrote a political colleague:

"When I accepted the office I now hold, it was under full persuasion that from similarity of thinking, combined with personal good will, I would have the firm support of Mr. Madison. I mean, first, the wisdom of funding the debt; second, the unwisdom of discriminating between original and present [bond] holders; third, the wisdom of assuming state debts...under these circumstances you will naturally imagine that it must have been a cause of surprise to me when I was informed that it was Mr. Madison's intention to oppose my plan..."[1]

General Philip Schuyler, one of the wealthiest and most powerful men in the state. Several years earlier, Schuyler had been elected US senator from New York. The Constitution called for US senators to be elected by state legislatures—a law that did not change until the twentieth century.

Opposed to Schuyler was a political faction, or group, headed by Governor George Clinton. Clinton disliked Schuyler and his son-in law Hamilton. About the same time as Washington's inauguration, Hamilton had led an effort to defeat Clinton when he ran for governor of New York. Although the effort failed, Clinton realized that he needed more political friends to survive the next challenge.

Aaron Burr's growing reputation as a lawyer had brought him to Clinton's attention. Soon after he was reelected, Clinton appointed Burr as attorney general of New York. This was the state's highest legal officer. As a reward for loyally serving him, Governor Clinton asked Burr to run against Schuyler for the US Senate.

Burr proved to be a very successful campaigner and an astute politician. He had never held high office, but this did not stop him from running a good campaign. For example, Burr was a strong supporter of increased spending for the army to guard the frontier, which included western New York. As a local newspaper had written during Burr's election race, "If any unusual concern of the state should require a prompt and active governor, it will probably be a threatened frontier. For war and negotiation this candidate [Burr] is known to be happily qualified."[2]

Burr's race was successful, and by a vote in the state Legislature of 32–27, he became a US senator in 1791. Shortly afterward, Burr met with Madison and Jefferson in New York. Both leaders had recognized Burr as an up-and-coming political leader. Hamilton, according to historian Nancy Isenberg, now worried that Jefferson and Madison were enlisting Burr against him.[3]

The local press also saw Burr as a moderate, not beholden to either the Schuyler or Clinton factions. His political power seemed to be increasing in New York, while Hamilton, who had backed the losing candidate, Schuyler, seemed to be losing power.

Hamilton strongly opposed Burr. During their years in the courtroom, he had developed a very negative opinion of Burr. At the time, letter writing played an important role in political campaigns. Letters also appeared in local newspapers, signed by anonymous writers, even though political insiders often knew their identities. Hamilton led such a campaign against Burr.

According to historian Nancy Isenberg, "Hamilton's personal attacks against Burr were consistent, and they all began with his three characterizations in the early 1790s: devoid of principles... privately reckless [in his finances] yet personally powerful... because he was 'bold, enterprising and intriguing....'"[4]

Public and Private

About the same time that Hamilton and Burr were clashing over the Senate seat, the secretary of the treasury issued his *Report on Manufactures*. He had taken on this project at the request of the House of Representatives. Hamilton had observed the beginnings of the Industrial Revolution in Great Britain, where thousands of people were moving from the countryside into growing cities to work in factories. There, they operated huge looms that produced cotton cloth or ran machines that turned out pottery. Much of England's wealth now depended on manufacturing.

Hamilton believed that a similar transition could occur in the United States with the help of the federal government. Although the nation was largely agricultural, Hamilton foresaw the day when industry might grow across the country. Unfortunately, his report drew the criticism of political leaders like Jefferson and Madison.

Shortly after the nation's founding, Aaron Burr pursued a political career in New York, where he served as a US senator. He later became a state representative.

They represented agricultural Virginia, not urban New York. And they were convinced that manufacturing would destroy the livelihoods of small farmers and plantation owners. By contrast, Hamilton believed that manufacturing centers would create new markets for farm products.

He said the following in his report:

"—Manufacturing institutions contribute to augment the general stock of industry and production. In places where those institutions prevail, besides the persons regularly engaged in them, they afford occasional and extra employment to industrious individuals and families, who are willing to devote the leisure resulting from the intermissions of their ordinary pursuits to [other] labors…The [farmer] himself experiences a new source of profit and support from the increased industry of his wife and daughters…."[5]

While Hamilton was doing his work in government, his private life seemed to be falling apart. One evening in 1791, a woman came to Hamilton's home seeking his financial assistance. His fame had brought her there, she said, and his reputation for helping others. He agreed to meet this woman, named Maria Reynolds, at her home the next day and give her a small amount of money. That meeting turned into a physical relationship between the two—a married secretary of treasury and a married woman. Reynolds was just twenty-three years old.

> *"Manufacturing institutions contribute to augment the general stock of industry and production."*
> — Alexander Hamilton

Aaron Burr and Dolley Payne

Dolley Payne lived in Philadelphia, the nation's capital. During a yellow fever epidemic in 1793, she had lost her husband, John Todd, and one of her sons. Aaron Burr knew Payne and provided her with legal advice after she became a widow. He also introduced her to James Madison, a widower, who was much older than Dolley. Eventually, the two married.

In 1808, Dolley Madison's husband was elected president, making her first lady. She gained a reputation as a highly successful hostess, much more outgoing than her husband. In the War of 1812, Dolley Madison rescued a famous portrait of George Washington from the White House in Washington, DC, just before the British burned it.

Apparently, Reynolds's husband, James, knew all about the relationship. Indeed, he had encouraged her to seek out Hamilton. Eventually Reynolds and her husband threatened to tell Hamilton's wife, unless he gave them a large sum of money. He handed over a thousand dollars, almost a third of what he earned from his job in government.

Meanwhile, James Reynolds had already been arrested for another crime. Reynolds hoped to gain his release by accusing Hamilton of giving him privileged information to help in his land speculations. Information about this accusation had come to the attention of Senator James Monroe of Virginia and two of his colleagues. The political officials asked to meet with Hamilton about the issue.

During the meeting, Hamilton admitted that he knew Reynolds but had not worked with him on illegal land

Dolley Payne lost her husband, John Todd, during an epidemic in Philadelphia, but Aaron Burr introduced her to his friend James Madison. He became her husband and the fourth president.

Alexander Hamilton built a magnificent home, overlooking the Hudson River, in northern Manhattan.

speculations. Instead, Hamilton told them that he had paid Reynolds money not to publicize an affair with Maria Reynolds.

Monroe and his two associates believed Hamilton. As Monroe put it: "We left under an impression our suspicions were removed."[6] They promised not to go public with the information. However, it eventually came out five years later—almost costing Hamilton his marriage to Betsey Schuyler.

POLITICAL CONFLICT

In 1792, George Washington easily won reelection as president, with John Adams as his vice president. But the political atmosphere in the United States was changing. While Washington tried to remain above politics, he worried that political conflict was increasing and might only grow much worse.

Political Clashes

On one side were the Federalists, led by Alexander Hamilton. On the other were the Democratic-Republicans led by Thomas Jefferson and James Madison. Each political party had its own clubs and newspapers, which fought elections and spread rumors about opposing candidates.

Aaron Burr at first seemed to move back and forth between both parties. But by 1793, it was clear that he was a Republican supporter. Whether he made the choice because of his own strong principles or his political ambition, no one knows. But both Burr and Hamilton shared an ambition to wield power and influence as national political leaders.

Meanwhile, the political parties clashed over events in Europe and their impact on the United States. In France, King

Caricature of Aaron Burr

In 1795, an unknown author published a poem making fun of Republican leaders and Aaron Burr especially. The poem says a lot about Burr's physical appearance and thirst for power. Today, political leaders continue to face public criticism.

The poem follows:

"Next...the courtly Burr is seen.
With piercing look, and ever varying mien;
Tho' small his stature, yet his well-known name,
Shines with full splendor on the rolls of fame;
Go search the records of intrigue, and find
To what debasement sinks the human mind
How far 'tis possible for man to go,
Where interest sways and passions urge the blow...."[1]

Louis XVI and his wife, Marie Antoinette, were overthrown and imprisoned by a radical, revolutionary government in the early 1790s. Republicans applauded the end to a tyrannical government, while Federalists feared bloodshed and chaos in France might spread to the United States. In early 1793, the king was executed, and Federalist fears seemed to have been well founded.

European governments, like Great Britain, declared war against France. But the United States remained neutral during the conflict. Nevertheless, the British navy decided to punish the United States by seizing more than 150 of its merchant ships. The British also seized American sailors and forced them to serve in the British navy—a practice called impressment.

King Louis XVI supported America through the revolution, but he bankrupted France to do so. This led to the French Revolution and the king's overthrow in 1789.

The French people blamed Queen Marie Antoinette, Louis XVI's Austrian wife, for many of the country's misfortunes.

During the 1790s, Pennsylvania farmers rebelled against a whiskey tax that Alexander Hamilton proposed. Hamilton led an army to put down the rebellion.

The Whiskey Rebellion

As treasury secretary, Hamilton had proposed a tax on whiskey, in part to help pay the costs of running the federal government. In western Pennsylvania, farmers rebelled against the tax. They used part of their wheat crops to make whiskey and recognized that the tax would cut into their profits. Threatened by the rebellious farmers, federal tax collectors asked Washington to call up the militia to put down the rebellion.

At first reluctant to call out the militia, Washington finally decided to act in late 1794. "If the laws are to be trampled," he said, "and a minority is to dictate to the majority, there is an end at one stroke to republican government."[2]

Washington asked Hamilton to join him in leading the militia into Pennsylvania. Eventually, the leaders of the rebellion fled in the face of the twelve-thousand-strong militia, and the revolt ended.

In 1794, President Washington appointed John Jay, a justice of the Supreme Court, to travel to England to negotiate a treaty with the British, ending their attacks on America's shipping and impressment of its sailors. While Jay persuaded the British to agree to American neutrality, England did not implement a provision to stop impressment, and American merchant shipping had very little protection.

The Jay Treaty became another source of conflict between Republicans and Federalists. It also increased the tensions between Hamilton and Burr. Hamilton supported the treaty and his friend John Jay, while Burr and other Republicans strongly opposed it. The treaty eventually passed with Federalist support in 1795.

A Change in Political Fortunes

After the Whiskey Rebellion, Hamilton told President Washington he planned to step down as treasury secretary. Public service had exhausted Hamilton and prevented him from earning much money to support his family. Upon Hamilton's return to New York in 1795, he attended a large dinner celebration given in his honor.

Many of the city's business leaders appreciated what Hamilton had done to safeguard the financial stability of the young United States. President Washington had also been pleased. As he wrote to Hamilton, "In every relationship which you have borne to me, I have found that my confidence in your talents, exertions and integrity has been well placed."[3]

> *"In every relationship which you have borne to me, I have found that my confidence in your talents, exertions and integrity has been well placed."*
> — George Washington

While Hamilton's career never seemed more successful, Aaron Burr had experienced some bad luck. Long involved in land speculation, Burr's investments had suffered. He was finally forced to sell off the furniture at his magnificent home in Lower Manhattan and eventually sold the estate to pay his debts. In 1794, his beloved wife, Theodosia, died from stomach cancer.

But Burr continued politicking. In 1796, President Washington announced that he was retiring at the end of his second term. He set a precedent followed by every president, until Franklin Roosevelt in 1940, of serving no more than two terms in office. Washington's logical successor was his vice president, John Adams.

Burr, however, hoped that Thomas Jefferson would run for president. And Burr also believed that he would be an excellent choice for the Republican vice president. Burr was popular in many parts of New York and New England and also had support in the South. Hamilton, meanwhile, did not support Vice President Adams. He tried to gather support for another Federalist, Thomas Pinckney of South Carolina.

The election results disappointed both Hamilton and Burr. Adams won the presidential election with the most electoral votes, and Pinckney became vice president. Aaron Burr, running as a Republican, had finished behind Pinckney in the vice presidential race.

Why hadn't Hamilton run for president? As biographer Ron Chernow explained, John Adams considered himself the heir apparent, or natural successor, to Washington. Chernow wrote that, unlike Washington, Hamilton was not prone to compromise or consensus building…Hamilton had no special interest in echoing popular preferences…[he was] much too avowedly elitist to become president."[4]

Nevertheless, Hamilton always had the full trust and confidence of George Washington. In fact, he helped to write Washington's farewell address to the American people when he left office in 1797. In this address, Washington talked about his fears of factions, that is, political groups or subsets. He also urged agricultural interests and industrial interests to work together for the sake of a stronger American economy. In addition, Washington warned political leaders to remain neutral and to stay out of European affairs. Jefferson and Madison, however, were strong supporters of the French Revolution.

Two Very Different Scandals

Men who served in the government did not receive high salaries, and Hamilton was no exception. When he returned to New York, Hamilton hoped to resume his law practice and find some high-paying clients. This would help him support his wife and children. But even after leaving Washington's administration, Hamilton found himself the constant target of attacks from the Republican politicians. They accused him of trying to influence the Adams administration, even though he no longer served in it.

Once Adams replaced Washington as president, Hamilton now found himself attacked by members of his own party. Adams knew that Hamilton had not supported him for president and totally excluded him from any advisory role in the new administration.

In 1797, Hamilton also had to deal with a scandal in both his political and personal life. Although James Monroe had promised Hamilton several years earlier not to release any of his letters to Maria Reynolds, somehow they reached the newspapers. The press had a field day accusing Hamilton of giving Reynolds's husband information to profit from land speculation.

To counter these charges, Hamilton wrote a long explanation of his relationship with Maria Reynolds. Although his admission to having an affair profoundly hurt his wife, Elizabeth, it clearly challenged any charges that might have been made against Hamilton for using his political office improperly.

But Hamilton was still convinced that Monroe had lied to him and released the letters. In a meeting with Monroe, Hamilton accused him of releasing the documents to the press. When Monroe denied this charge, Hamilton said, "Your representation is totally false." The two men arose from their chairs, and Monroe accused Hamilton of being a "scoundrel." Hamilton responded, "I will meet you like a gentleman." In other words, he challenged Monroe to a duel.[5]

During the following year, both men exchanged letters with accusations against each other that might have led to a duel. Eventually, Monroe asked for aid from Aaron Burr, a political ally. He showed Burr the letters to and from Hamilton. Burr suggested that Monroe destroy the correspondence and put an end to the conflict. He also remained on friendly enough terms with Hamilton to act as a neutral party, trying to help both sides to avoid a duel that might prove fatal. As Chernow wrote, Burr "was the one upright actor in the whole affair."[6] No duel between Monroe and Hamilton ever occurred.

While Burr was trying to mediate the conflict between Hamilton and Monroe, he had become involved in a scandal of his own. Burr had left the US Senate and won an election to the New York State legislature. There, he became involved in a shady land deal. Always in need of money, Burr had received a large tract of land in Pennsylvania and New York from a group of foreign investors. Burr had not put down any money for the property, but he had promised to change the laws in New York to allow foreigners to purchase more land in the future.

Hamilton's brother-in-law, John Barker Church, accused Burr of taking a bribe to change the law. When Burr heard about this accusation, he challenged Church to a duel. In 1798, the two men went out to a dueling ground near Hoboken, New Jersey. Burr's shot went wide, but Church's bullet hit a button on Burr's coat. Both men were unharmed, and Church

> *"That it shall and may be lawful for the said company to employ all such surplus capital as may accrue to the said company in the purchase of public or other stock, or in any other money transactions or operations...for the sole benefit of the said company."*[7]
>
> — **Aaron Burr**

decided to end the duel and apologize to Burr.

Soon afterward, Burr became involved in another project that appeared to be designed to enrich him. Manhattan needed larger supplies of fresh water to serve its growing number of inhabitants. Burr decided to lead a company that would provide these supplies. The company would build pipes channeling clean water from the Bronx River, north of the city, into Manhattan. Then Burr convinced the state legislature to charter the company, allowing it to use any surplus funds raised from selling stock to become deposits in a new bank.

There, the funds could be available as loans for Burr and his Republican friends to use in political campaigns or land speculation.

THE ELECTION OF 1800

In the winter of 1799, the body of a woman was discovered in a well owned by the Manhattan Company. Her name was Gulielma Sands, and she'd lived in a nearby boardinghouse. Sands had been strangled and then dropped into the well to hide her body.

A Big Case for Burr

Levi Weeks, who also lived in the boarding house, had identified the body. A carpenter, Weeks had decided to marry Sands, according to people acquainted with him. Rumors began to swirl that Sands had refused to marry Weeks, and he had retaliated by murdering her. One newspaper ran the headline: "HORRID MURDER! BY HANDS OF LOVER!"[1]

The authorities put Weeks in prison and prepared to prosecute him for murder. Weeks, whose brother was a prominent New York builder, hired Aaron Burr to defend him. The prosecutor was Cadwallader David Colden, member of a prominent New York family.

As the prosecution opened, Colden presented twenty-four witnesses who testified about the romance between Weeks and

Sands. But several of the witnesses seemed unable to present any direct evidence of their relationship, while others seemed to hold a grudge against Weeks. The testimony, therefore, seemed unsupported by any hard facts.

When Burr presented his defense, he pointed out that Weeks had been having dinner when Sands was killed. Burr also suggested that instead of Sands breaking up with Weeks, it might have been the other way around. As a result, Sands may have killed herself. The jury agreed with the evidence Burr had presented. After deliberating for only a few minutes, they found Weeks not guilty. Burr's reputation had never soared any higher, but he had plans to take it up a notch.

The Campaign for President

In 1800, the nation would hold another presidential election. President John Adams had decided to run for a second term. However, his popularity had greatly declined since he had taken office in 1797. He could partly blame this on the Alien and Sedition Acts that his party, the Federalists, had championed.

Federalists feared that revolutionary ideas from France might travel to the United States and jeopardize the nation's stability. Therefore, they tried to lengthen the amount of time that an immigrant from Europe must wait to become an American citizen—the Alien Act. And the Sedition Act tried to restrict the ideas that appeared in newspapers, if they appeared to challenge the political system.

The acts upset the Republicans because some of their supporters were new immigrants, and many members of their party supported the French Revolution. They also believed that the Sedition Act restricted freedom of speech, a right safeguarded by the US Constitution. The Republicans were planning to run Thomas Jefferson, an opponent of the Alien and Sedition Acts,

Elected second US president in 1796, John Adams failed to win a second term. His lack of political skills and opposition from Hamilton and Thomas Jefferson contributed to the loss.

as their presidential candidate in 1800. He had come close to defeating Adams in 1796, but at this time, Jefferson seemed to have an even better chance of becoming president.

The Republicans expected to win in the southern and western states, while the Federalists had a majority in New England and the Middle Atlantic states. New York had long been a Federalist stronghold. The Federalists were huge supporters of business and trade—both centered in New York City.

Still, Burr believed that with some hard work, he might reverse the Federalist majority in New York. After joining the New York legislature in 1797, Burr had supported many new bills that appealed to working people. These included lower taxes for middle- and low-income people. Therefore, they tended to support him.

In addition, Burr had also made a systematic study of the voting patterns across the state. He sent Republican campaign workers to various areas trying to persuade Federalist voters to support Republican candidates. In New York City, Burr's home became an election headquarters for the Republicans. And Burr traveled widely across New York speaking to groups of potential voters. His daughter Theodosia often accompanied him.

Born in 1783, Theodosia Burr was the only child of Aaron and his wife, Theodosia Bartow Burr. Aaron Burr wanted his daughter to have the same education that boys received, much like his wife had. In addition to the subjects reserved for girls, such as music and French, young Theodosia studied arithmetic, Latin, Greek, and writing. She would go on to play an important role in managing her father's finances and running his home.

In May, the Republicans met in Philadelphia to select their candidates for president and vice president. Jefferson was a natural choice for president. While former governor Clinton was an attractive choice for vice president, many delegates also favored Burr. They recognized how much he was doing to win

New York for the Republicans, and delegates wanted a New Yorker with Burr's political expertise and popularity to balance Jefferson, a southerner.

The results of the presidential election could not have been closer:

Jefferson   73 electoral votes
Burr   73 electoral votes
Adams   65 electoral votes
Pinckney   64 electoral votes

Therefore, there was no clear winner. Burr could have decided at this point to ask some of his electors to support Jefferson. But he did not, probably because he wanted to be president himself. At first, some Federalists wanted to support Burr and put their electoral votes behind him. Burr, for some of them, seemed a better choice than Jefferson.

However, Alexander Hamilton, who was the leader of the Federalist Party, wrote to some of its members, "For heaven's sake let not the Federalist party be responsible for the elevation of this man."[2] Hamilton went even further, suggesting that Burr as president might bring down the American Republic. As author Nancy Issenberg wrote, "Hamilton was accusing Burr of being unbalanced, of lacking moral values, of behaving as a political chameleon, and of despising democracy, while playing it for all it was worth."[3]

> "For heaven's sake let not the Federalist party be responsible for the elevation of this man."
> — Alexander Hamilton

Under the Constitution, if the Electoral College deadlocks, then the House of Representatives must decide the presidential election. In the House, voting began on February 11, 1801. The balloting went on for several days. Jefferson had won eight states, while

Burr had only six, and in two states an even amount of votes went to both candidates.

Finally, Jefferson began to pick up support among several states. He eventually won ten states out of sixteen, with only four for Burr. It was enough for Jefferson to become America's third president. Burr became vice president.

The Decline of Burr's Political Career

Burr had won the second most powerful position in the federal government. But he soon discovered that he actually had no

Theodosia Burr

Over the years Theodosia Burr and her father carried on a rich correspondence, which included thousands of letters. Theodosia also became her father's closest confidante. Since Burr did not remarry after his wife died, his daughter acted as his hostess at their home in Richmond Hill in Lower Manhattan.

In 1801, Theodosia married Joseph Alston, a successful South Carolina planter and later governor of the state. Their only son, Aaron Burr Alston, was born in 1802 but died at age ten from malaria.

Aaron Burr later moved to Europe, but his daughter remained in the United States and acted as a financial advisor, helping him safeguard his wealth. However, Theodosia did not have good health. In December 1812, she was traveling aboard the ship *Patriot* between Charleston, South Carolina, and New York. During the journey, the ship sank and everyone on board drowned. For Aaron Burr, the death of his daughter was a loss from which he may have never recovered.

Named after her mother, Theodosia Burr was not only Aaron Burr's daughter but also his closest advisor and one of the few people he trusted to improve his political career.

The Twelfth Amendment

In 1804, Congress passed the Twelfth Amendment to the Constitution in order to avoid what had occurred in the election of 1800. That is, the electors at the Electoral College would vote for president and vice president separately. The amendment reads:

"The Electors shall meet in their respective States and vote by ballot for President and Vice President...they shall name in their ballots the person voted for as President, and in distinct ballots the person voted for as Vice-President, and they shall make distinct lists of all persons voted for as President, and of all persons voted for as Vice-President, and of the number of votes for each...."

power at all. Jefferson ignored him and refused to consider most of Burr's suggestions for the new administration.

Back in New York, political leaders who had opposed Burr jumped on the chance to discredit him now that he seemed to have so little power. Rumors circulated about Burr's projects and private life. He asked President Jefferson to intervene and show support for his vice president, but Jefferson refused to do anything.

In New York, the rumors about Burr increased. Pamphlets circulated written by political opponents accusing Burr of being a tyrant, "confessed in all his villainy."[4] He was also accused of carrying on affairs with numerous women. Meanwhile, he continued in his role as vice president, presiding over deliberations in the Senate, which was part of his job. But there was little contact between Burr and President Jefferson.

As Burr wrote his son-in-law, "I dine with the president about once a fortnight, and now and then meet ministers in the street. They are all very busy: quite men of business. The Senate and the vice president are content with each and move on with courtesy."[5]

Meanwhile, Republicans opposed to Burr were working hard to ensure that he would not be renominated for vice president in 1804. But Burr did not intend to give them the chance to humiliate him. That same year, he announced his plan to run for governor of New York and resign as vice president.

Hamilton, of course, strongly opposed Burr's campaign for governor. But Burr had the support of many working class New Yorkers because he supported a law that would reduce the amount of property a New Yorker needed to own to qualify to vote.

During Burr's campaign, his supporters focused on his outstanding military record during the American Revolution. They called him a "self-made man," not someone with inherited wealth. They also championed him as someone who had risen to the top on his own merit, not because of his family connections.

> "General Hamilton did not oppose Mr. Burr because he was a democrat...but because HE HAD NO PRINCIPLE, either in morals or in politics. The sum and substance of his language was that no party could trust him."[6]
> — American Citizen

But it was not enough. Hamilton led the opposition against him, calling Burr a "dangerous man," not fit for "the reins of government," and "despicable."[7] On election day, Burr was overwhelmed and lost in a landslide. For a man who had risen so high, Burr had now reached the lowest point in his career.

DECLINE AND FALL

"Once Jefferson became president, Hamilton, forty-six, began to fade from public view," wrote Ron Chernow, "an abrupt fall for a man whose rise had been so spectacular."[1] He was no longer George Washington's right-hand man, treasury secretary, or the leader of the Federalist Party. Instead, Hamilton began to turn his attention more and more to his family—his wife and his seven children.

Hamilton started construction on a new home in the northern part of Manhattan Island, overlooking the Hudson River. Called the Grange, it was a beautiful two-story house, painted white and yellow. Like other spacious homes at that time, the Grange had magnificent gardens filled with flowers and trees.

Philip Hamilton's Fate: A Warning to Alexander

Unfortunately, the Grange had not yet been completed when Hamilton lost his oldest son, Philip. The tragic event can be traced to a man named George Eacker, who'd presented a Fourth of July address that seemed to insult Alexander Hamilton. Later that year, Philip and a friend saw Eacker at the theater. During the play, they walked up to Eacker, with Philip loudly criticizing him. Then the three men left to continue their argument in the lobby.

Eacker immediately commented that it was "too abominable to be publicly insulted by a set of rascals." Men of that period considered "rascal" to be just as insulting as "despicable" and cause for a duel. When they had finished their argument and went back to the play, Eacker said, "I expect to hear from you." Both Eacker and his friend answered, "You shall."[2] This heated argument eventually led to a duel between Hamilton and Eacker in 1800.

The Duel That Killed Philip Hamilton

Philip Hamilton met Eacker on a dueling ground in New Jersey the day after their confrontation at the theater. At first the two men refused to fire at each other. Then Eacker lifted his weapon and fired a fatal shot into Hamilton's right hip and through his body. Hamilton intentionally fired his shot high, not intending to hit Eacker.

Hamilton was lifted from the dueling ground, placed in a boat and carried across the Hudson River. Although the city's finest physicians were called to treat Hamilton, he died at his parents' home. Alexander Hamilton's entire life changed immediately, and his despair overcame him. As a friend of Hamilton recalled, "The scene I was present at when Mrs. Hamilton came to see her son on his deathbed…and when she met her husband and son in one room beggars all description." The man later added, "Never did I see a man so completely overwhelmed with grief as Hamilton has been."[3]

In 1801, a single word, "rascal," had triggered a series of reactions leading to the killing of Philip Hamilton. Three years later, another word, "despicable," would result in his father, Alexander Hamilton, suffering the same fate.

The tinder for the fire had been laid years earlier. Burr and Hamilton always had a competitive rivalry. In earlier years, Burr had probably envied Hamilton because of his close relationship with George Washington, a position that Burr himself wanted. Later, Burr had then taken leadership of the Republican Party in New York. With his expertise as a campaign organizer, he had assured Jefferson's eventual victory in the election of 1800.

After the duel, Alexander Hamilton was rowed across the Hudson River and brought to his Manhattan home, the Grange, where he died.

When some of the Federalists talked about supporting Burr for president, Hamilton had denounced the man as someone with no principles. New York politics was a small arena, and word of Hamilton's criticism surely got back to Burr. What's more, Hamilton made no attempt to hide his contempt for Burr as a man and a politician.

Meanwhile, Burr, in competing with Jefferson for the presidency, had earned the lasting dislike of the new president of the United States. In fact, Jefferson planned to replace Burr as vice president in 1804. As a result, Burr found himself as a man with few allies.

Then, Burr had decided to run for governor of New York in 1804, hoping to rebuild his political power. At first, Burr seemed to be heading toward victory. But Hamilton worked as hard as possible to defeat him. One Burr supporter explained that Hamilton "opposed the election of Colonel Burr with an ardor bordering on fanaticism."[4] Reports and rumors about Burr's morals also hurt his chances of being elected, and the result was a landslide defeat at the polls. One of Burr's friends believed that "If General Hamilton had not opposed Colonel Burr, I have very little doubt he would have been elected governor of New York."[5]

> *"If General Hamilton had not opposed Colonel Burr, I have very little doubt he would have been elected governor of New York."*

Following the election, Burr was angry. Once again, Hamilton had attacked and defeated him. Then came word that Hamilton and another man, James Kent, had made extremely negative comments about Burr at a private dinner. This information appeared in a letter written by Dr. Charles Cooper, who overheard the conversation. In addition, Cooper wrote that he "could detail…a still more despicable opinion which General Hamilton had expressed of Mr. Burr."[6]

The letter by Dr. Cooper appeared in a New York newspaper. When Burr read it, the report of Hamilton's remarks made him even angrier. On June 18, Burr wrote a letter to Hamilton demanding that he explain himself and the use of the word "despicable."

Hamilton refused for several reasons. He did not want his courage called into question. That would be an enormous black mark on his reputation. In addition, Hamilton could foresee a day when the United States might need to put another army in the field to defeat an enemy, possibly even the British again. The British ran Canada and could partner with Native Americans on the frontier to stop any westward expansion by Americans. If war came, Hamilton wanted to lead an army against the British, but this would be impossible if he backed away from a duel against Aaron Burr.

Hamilton had already been involved in six previous duels, but only in the early stages, as an advisor or a second. He had never fought a duel. But this time he told a friend that he was "convinced that nothing would satisfy the malice of Burr but the sacrifice of his [Hamilton's] life."[7] In his response to Burr's letter, Hamilton refused to admit to anything that might be "despicable." Burr responded in the same tone, bringing the men closer to a duel.

Hamilton's next letter was just as strongly worded. In response, Burr said that he had taken Hamilton's insults over the years "till it approached humiliation."[8] According to Hamilton's biographer, Ron Chernow, "By this point, Burr was clearly spoiling for a fight." Burr was a very good shot and intended to fire his bullet during the duel. In fact, some of Burr's friends considered it "more like an assassination than a duel."[9]

On June 27, 1804, William Van Ness, Burr's second, delivered to Nathaniel Pendleton, Hamilton's second, the expected request for a duel. Hamilton planned to follow the same course of action that his son, Philip, had used, firing high. He hoped that Burr might do the same thing. But Burr had decided to kill Hamilton. And that was exactly the result of their famous duel.

The Results of Burr's Decision

Burr had proven his courage in the duel with Alexander Hamilton. But what else had he achieved? The states of New York and New Jersey both indicted him for murder for dueling. As a result, Burr could no longer remain at his home without risking trial and imprisonment. He fled from the North to live with a friend, Pierce Butler, in Georgia. There, dueling was considered no more than an honorable undertaking among gentlemen.

But Burr eventually returned to Washington, DC, where he took up his duties again as vice president. These duties included presiding over the United States Senate, but he continued to have very little contact with President Jefferson. By this time, Jefferson had been reelected, with New York governor George Clinton elected vice president. Burr's political career was over. On his last day in the Senate, he delivered a farewell address that at least some members found very moving.

Aaron Burr's focus now turned westward. In 1803, President Jefferson had purchased the Louisiana Territory from France for $15 million. This territory more than doubled the size of the United States. Burr hoped that land speculation there might pay off his debts and replenish his fortune. In fact, a friend of Burr, General James Wilkinson, had been appointed governor of the Louisiana Territory, with headquarters in New Orleans. Burr

Reactions to Burr's Last Speech

Senator Samuel Mitchill of New York said, "I never experienced anything of the kind so affecting as this parting scene…My colleague, General Smith, stout and manly as he is, wept profusely as I did. He laid his head upon his table and did not recover from his emotion for a quarter of an hour or more. And for myself, though it is more than three hours since Burr went away, I have scarcely recovered my habitual calmness. Several gentlemen came up to me to talk about this extraordinary scene, but I was obliged to turn away and decline all conversation."[10]

thought his relationship with Wilkinson might open the door to acquiring some new properties.

In 1805, Burr took a long journey of about 3,000 miles (4,828 km) down the Ohio and Mississippi rivers and stopped along the way in New Orleans. The new Louisiana Territory bordered lands controlled by the Spanish government. Tensions between Spain and the United States had grown, as both sides seemed to be expecting the outbreak of war. If war came, Burr hoped to lead an expedition to conquer some of the Spanish lands.

Burr followed up his first trip with a second expedition in 1806, hoping to find some land in the West to purchase and sell to settlers. Meanwhile, rumors had begun to fly that Burr planned something far greater than simply buying property. He wanted to start a revolution among the states along the Alleghany Mountains and form an independent republic with himself as its head.

The duel left Aaron Burr's reputation in tatters, so he joined a conspiracy to lead the western states out of the union. The plot was discovered, leading to Burr's trial for treason.

One newspaper stated, "It is discovered beyond the possibility of doubt, that there has been a dangerous and daring conspiracy afoot...carried on by those, and those exclusively, who style themselves 'the union of honest men'....*Aaron Burr*, the leader of the lawless conspirators, is notoriously known to be father of the...faction."[11] In fact, the plan became known as the Burr Conspiracy.

General Wilkinson feared that he might somehow be blamed for the conspiracy because of his friendship with Burr, according to Burr's biographer, Nancy Isenberg. Therefore, Wilkinson forged a report that supported the claims that Burr was planning to set himself up to lead a new nation. According to Wilkinson, he had read the report after it was printed for the public. But in reality, it was his own writing. The report "claimed that as many as 10,000 men had formed a powerful association, and planned to topple New Orleans, invade Mexico, and incite an insurrection capable of sending tremors far enough east to subvert the federal government." [12]

President Jefferson finally ordered Burr's arrest. And in 1807 in Richmond, Burr stood trial for treason—a charge of trying to undermine the United States government. Presiding over the trial was John Marshall, the chief justice of the Supreme Court. After listening to all the testimony, Marshall stated that there was not enough evidence to convict Burr. The next day, the jury reached their own verdict: "We of the jury say that Aaron Burr is not proved to be guilty

"We of the jury say that Aaron Burr is not proved to be guilty under the indictment by any evidence submitted to us. We, therefore, find him not guilty."

under the indictment by any evidence submitted to us. We, therefore, find him not guilty."[13]

But Burr's reputation had been destroyed. Soon afterward, he left the United States to live in Europe, and over the next five years, Burr moved around the continent, finally settling in England. Eventually, he returned to the United States in 1812. Burr lived his remaining years in retirement, far from public service, dying in 1836.

Hamilton and Burr

Great political leaders, like the rest of us, are not perfect people. Even men like Alexander Hamilton and Aaron Burr had their faults. Both men were courageous war heroes, serving the country bravely during the American Revolution. Hamilton even became one of General George Washington's closest aides. Hamilton and Burr later achieved great success in their legal careers. And they became powerful political leaders both in New York and on the national stage.

Hamilton was the leader of the Federalist Party, Burr a leader of the Republican Party. And he almost became president in the election of 1800. Yet for all of their success, both men also engaged in secret romantic relationships. In addition, Burr became involved in land speculation that kept him continuously in debt. He was also not above skirting the law as a public official. He helped his friends, and they enabled him to participate in shady land deals.

Both men were also passionate in their beliefs, which led them into a years-long rivalry and bitter hatred that finally ended on the dueling ground. Dueling in the early nineteenth century was a method used by men of the upper classes to prove their manhood and courage. But both Hamilton and Burr had proven their courage many times before.

What led them to the most famous duel in American history? Politics, hatred, uncontrollable passions, and an overriding need for each man to prove that he was right. The result was an American tragedy.

1755

Alexander Hamilton is born on the island of Nevis.

1756

Aaron Burr is born in New Jersey.

1756–1763

French and Indian War rages on in North America.

1772

Burr graduates from Princeton.

1773

Hamilton arrives in New York City.

1774

Burr attends law school; Hamilton attends college.

1775

American Revolution begins in Massachusetts.
Burr leaves law school to join Continental army.
Burr joins American expedition to Canada.

1776

Burr and Hamilton fight British troops in New York.
Hamilton fights in Battle of Trenton, Princeton.
Hamilton becomes General Washington's aide.

1777

Hamilton fights at Battle of Brandywine.

1778

Burr and Hamilton fight at Battle of Monmouth.

1780

Hamilton marries Elizabeth Schuyler.

1781

Hamilton fights at Battle of Yorktown.

1782

Burr marries Theodosia Prevost.

1783

Hamilton and Burr both live in New York and practice law.

1787

Hamilton attends Constitutional Convention.

1788

Hamilton, Jay, and Madison write Federalist Papers.

1789

Hamilton becomes treasury secretary.
George Washington becomes president.

1791

Burr becomes a US senator.
Whiskey Rebellion breaks out.

1792

Washington is elected to second term as president.

1794

Theodosia Burr dies.

1797

John Adams becomes president.

1800

Burr and Jefferson run for president.

1801

Jefferson becomes president; Burr is vice president.

1803

Jefferson makes Louisiana Purchase.

1804

Burr runs for governor of New York.
Burr kills Hamilton in duel.

1805

Burr retires as vice president.

1807

Burr tried for treason.

1808

Burr flees to Europe.

1812

Burr returns to United States.

1836

Burr dies.

INTRODUCTION

1. Ross Drake, "Duel!," *Smithsonian Magazine*, March 2004, https://www.smithsonianmag.com/history/duel-104161025/.
2. Ibid.

CHAPTER 1

Duel to the Death

1. John Sedgwick, *War of Two* (New York, NY: Random House, 2015), p. 341.
2. "The Funeral," Founders Online, July 14, 1804, https://founders.archives.gov/documents/Hamilton/01-26-02-0001-0271.

CHAPTER 2

Growing Up in the Colonies

1. John Sedgwick, *War of Two* (New York, NY: Random House, 2015), pp. 16–17.
2. Ibid., pp. 32–33.
3. Ibid., p. 35.

CHAPTER 3

The Cauldron of the Revolution

1. John Sedgwick, *War of Two* (New York, NY: Random House, 2015), p. 44.

2. Christopher Ward, *The War of the Revolution* (New York, NY: Macmillan, 1952), Vol. I, p. 178.
3. Ibid., p. 180.

CHAPTER 4

The World Turned Upside Down

1. Christopher Ward, *The War of the Revolution* (New York, NY: Macmillan, 1952), Vol. I, p. 348.
2. Ibid., p. 361.
3. John Sedgwick, *War of Two* (New York, NY: Random House, 2015), p. 93.
4. Ibid., pp. 94.
5. Ward, p. 731.
6. Sedgwick, p. 118.
7. Ward, p. 893.

CHAPTER 5

The Law and the Constitution

1. Nancy Isenberg, *Fallen Founder: The Life of Aaron Burr* (New York, NY: Penguin Books, 2007), p. 69.
2. John Sedgwick, *War of Two* (New York, NY: Random House, 2015), p. 139.
3. Ibid., p. 147.
4. Alexander Hamilton, *Federalist No. 6: Concerning Dangers from Dissensions Between the States,* accessed December 17, 2017, http://www.foundingfathers. info/federalistpapers/fed06.htm.

CHAPTER 6
The Indispensable Man

1. Charles Sellers, *As It Happened: A History of the United States* (New York, NY: McGraw Hill, 1975), p. 249.
2. Nancy Isenberg, *Fallen Founder: The Life of Aaron Burr* (New York, NY: Penguin Books, 2007), p. 109.
3. Ibid., pp. 105–107.
4. Ibid., p. 119.
5. Harold Syrett, "Alexander Hamilton, Report on Manufactures," *The Papers of Alexander Hamilton, vol.1,* New York, NY: Columbia University Press, 1961-1979.
6. Ron Chernow, *Alexander Hamilton* (New York, NY: Penguin Books, 2004), p. 416.

CHAPTER 7
Political Conflict

1. Nancy Isenberg, *Fallen Founder: The Life of Aaron Burr* (New York, NY: Penguin Books, 2007), p. 129.
2. John Sedgwick, *War of Two* (New York, NY: Random House, 2015), p. 242.
3. Ron Chernow, *Alexander Hamilton* (New York, NY: Penguin Books, 2004), p. 509.
4. Ibid., p. 473.

5. Ibid., p. 539.
6. Ibid., p. 541.
7. Sedgwick, p. 272.

CHAPTER 8

The Election of 1800

1. John Sedgwick, *War of Two* (New York, NY: Random House, 2015), p. 283.
2. Nancy Isenberg, *Fallen Founder: The Life of Aaron Burr* (New York, NY: Penguin Books, 2007), p. 211.
3. Ibid., p. 212.
4. Ibid., p. 231.
5. Ibid., p. 246.
6. Ron Chernow, *Alexander Hamilton* (New York, NY: Penguin Books, 2004), p. 674.
7. Isenberg, p. 257.

CHAPTER 9

Decline and Fall

1. Ron Chernow, *Alexander Hamilton* (New York, NY: Penguin Books, 2004), p. 640.
2. Ibid., p. 652.
3. Ibid., p. 655.
4. Ibid., p. 674.
5. Ibid., p. 677.
5. Ibid., pp. 680–681.
6. Ibid., p. 681.

7. Ibid., p. 685.
8. Ibid., 688.
9. Ibid., p. 688.
10. Nancy Isenberg, *Fallen Founder: The Life of Aaron Burr* (New York, NY: Penguin Books, 2007), p. 279.
11. Ibid., p. 271
12. Ibid., p. 312.
13. ibid., p. 362.

affair of honor A duel fought to preserve a man's honor.

Articles of Confederation A weak central government that governed the American states during the Revolution and most of the 1780s.

bateaux A large raft.

bonds Certificates of debt issued by the United States.

Burr Conspiracy A rumored attempt by Aaron Burr to establish an independent Western republic.

column A long line of troops.

Democratic-Republican Party One of two major American political parties in the early Republic.

Federalist Papers A series of letters written by Hamilton, Jay and Madison in support of the Constitution.

Federalist Party One of the two major political parties in the early American republic.

flank One end of an army's position.

impressment Illegal seizure of sailors from neutral ships.

Loyalists Americans who supported the British government.

parapet Walls of a fortification.

regiment A body of troops consisting of several companies.

seconds Friends of the duelists who ensured that the duel followed the rules.

Tories Another term for Loyalists.

treason Activities by a citizen designed to undermine his/her government.

trench Lines dug into the ground where soldiers could defend themselves.

BOOKS

Chernow, Ron. *Alexander Hamilton.* New York: Penguin Books, 2004.

Isenberg, Nancy. *Fallen Founder: Life of Aaron Burr.* New York: Viking, 2007.

Kent, Newmyer. *The Treason Trial of Aaron Burr.* New York: Cambridge University Press, 2012.

Sedgwick, John. *War of Two: Alexander Hamilton, Aaron Burr, and the Duel That Stunned The Nation.* New York: Berkley Books, 2015.

St. George, Judith. *The Duel,* New York: Viking, 2009.

WEBSITES

Hamilton The Musical
www.hamiltonbroadway.com
A discussion and information about the musical, Hamilton.

History Now
www.historynow.com
Information about the lives of Alexander Hamilton and Aaron Burr.

FILMS AND VIDEOS

Alexander Hamilton: American Experience (2006)
Alexander Hamilton (2007)
The Duel (2011)